THE ADVENTURES OF ALI & ALIR
AND THE AXES OF EVIL

OWL

THE ADVENTURES OF ALI & ALI
AND THE aXES OF EVIL

A *Divertimento* for Warlords

Marcus Youssef
Guillermo Verdecchia
Camyar Chai

Talonbooks
Vancouver

Copyright © 2005 Marcus Youssef, Guillermo Verdecchia, Camyar Chai

Talonbooks
P.O. Box 2076, Vancouver, British Columbia, Canada V6B 3S3
www.talonbooks.com

Typeset in Scala and printed and bound in Canada by AGMV Marquis.

First Printing: 2005

The publisher gratefully acknowledges the financial support of the Canada Council for the Arts; the Government of Canada through the Book Publishing Industry Development Program; and the Province of British Columbia through the British Columbia Arts Council for our publishing activities.

Library and Archives Canada Cataloguing in Publication

Youssef, Marcus
        The adventures of Ali & Ali and the Axes of evil : a divertimento for warloards / Marcus Youssef, Guillermo Verdecchia and Camyar Chai.

A play.
ISBN 0-88922-516-8

        1. War on Terrorism, 2001- —Drama. 2. Middle East—Politics and government—21st century—Drama. I. Verdecchia, Guillermo II. Chai, Camyar

III. Title.

PS8597.O89A79 2005   C812'.54
C2004-906439-8

The Adventures of Ali & Ali and the aXes of Evil was co-developed and co-produced by NeWorld Theatre and Cahoots Theatre Projects.

In 2004, it was presented at the Vancouver East Cultural Centre; at Theatre Passe Muraille in Toronto, and at Montréal, Arts Interculturel with the following cast:

Camyar Chai	Ali Hakim
	Dr. Mohandes Panir Ali Zia
Marcus Youssef	Ali Ababwa
Tom Butler	Tim, Duncan, Osama
Guillermo Verdecchia	Jean Paul Jacques Beauderrièredada

The show was later presented in Edmonton as part of the Magnetic North Festival at the Varscona Theatre with John Murphy in the roles of Tim, Duncan, and Osama.

These productions were stage managed by DK (David Kerr).

The set and costumes were designed by Marina Szijarto; lights by Sharon Huizinga; sound and music by Alejandro Verdecchia; properties by Rob Lewis; signs, graphics, and pillowcases by Richard Lawley; video by Andrew Laurenson (and friends).

The authors especially thank Tom Butler, DK, and John Murphy for their many contributions, suggestions, and improvements, not to mention sandwiches and drinks.

The authors also thank: Heather Brown, Mara Coward, Kathleen Duborg, Amanda Fritzlan, Yvonne Gall, Maryam Ghaeni, Tamsin Kelsey, Duncan Low, Alice Niwinsky, Carlo Proto, Jovanni Sy, and Jim Warren; as well as Norman Armour, See Seven, and the Vancouver Foundation; Rahul Varma, Laurel Sprengelmeyer, and Anisa Cameron at Teesri Duniya Theatre; the City of Vancouver, and the Canada Council for the Arts.

Portions of this manuscript were originally published in *CRANK Magazine*.

The stage is more or less bare. The rear wall is a vaguely tent-like structure, onto which video is projected throughout. There is a worn carpet centre stage and some laundry (socks, some underwear) drying on the set.

Music expressing the happiness of brown people in liberated zones plays as the audience enter and pass through the Ali and Ali security apparatus.[1]

Totally funky, vaguely Arabic-Persian-Indo-world-fusion-cuisine music kicks in. The sound of a crowd roaring rises and falls. It could be a rock concert.

VOICE OVER:

You've heard the rumours: fresh from their sold-out tour of East Monrovia and the jungle encampments of Congolese bauxite smugglers ... on their way to the unacknowledged detention centres of Axerbaijan ... They're here, they're live, and they've got a Korean! Are you ready Mogadishu? Butt out your cigars and wipe the buckets of sweat

---

1. Pre-show possibilities include videos of John Ashcroft, Attorney General of the United States of America, singing his original composition, "Let the Eagle Soar"; or of George W. Bush and Tony Blair singing Diana Ross and Lionel Richie's "Endless Love" (by Johan Söderberg) and/or "Gay Bar" (by Electric 6). Google them.

from your really black black brows, put your stumps and prostheses together and give a GREAT BIG CLASH OF CIVILIZATIONS WELCOME TO ALI AND ALI!

ALI & ALI enter.

ALI ABABWA:
We know you're not Somalia.

ALI HAKIM:
We know where we are.

ALI ABABWA:
We had a little trouble at the border.

ALI HAKIM:
No time to redo intro.

ALI ABABWA:
And we know how much you were looking forward to see us perform with a real-life Korean, as advertised in the intro, but we don't have one.

ALI HAKIM:
Friday Kim Chee. We lost him in Mogadishu.

They make the Agrabanian "Piña Majorca" gesture (lightly touching the forehead then looking up and raising hands as if to ward off something falling from above) to acknowledge his passing.

ALI HAKIM:
He had a "fishing" accident.

ALI ABABWA:
In Mogadishu.

ALI HAKIM:
One must be so careful with the daughter of a
heavily armed ... "general."

ALI ABABWA:
So we had to hire a new guy.

ALI HAKIM:
Come.

TIM enters.

ALI ABABWA:
Off!

TIM exits.

ALI HAKIM:
And now the show—

ALI ABABWA:
But Holy Hummus did they love us in Mogadishu,
huh? What a show. They were falling in the aisles,
hooting and screaming, killing themselves. Ali
Hakim told this joke—

ALI HAKIM:
Ali Ababwa let us do—

ALI ABABWA:

No seriously. It was great. You're so funny. In
Agraba, he was big star. Hey! You should tell them
the joke.

ALI HAKIM:

Not now. I don't think this is the sort of aud—

ALI ABABWA:

Oh, come on—do you remember what happened?
So we're in Mogadishu and Ali Hakim tells the
joke and everybody's laughing and suddenly the
Big Guy himself, Mr. Biggest Warlord, very slowly
he holds up this pistol and all the soldiers go quiet
'cause they're sure he's going to blow Ali's brains
out. And then—you won't believe what he said. He
says, "I like this joke." Just like that. And then he
fires pistol in the air and goes, "Tell it again."
Go on. Tell them.

ALI HAKIM doesn't want to.

Fine, I'll tell it. I'll mess it all up. OK, so, this fat
guy walks into the Arctic, he's Italian—

ALI HAKIM:

No no no! Stop! You're ruining it.

ALI HAKIM reluctantly finishes the joke.

So. There is—this pisshole ... in the desert. And
there is a warlord, taking a piss. Suddenly, a small
white man—yay high—with red hair comes, stand
beside warlord, also taking piss. Warlord, who
surprisingly for black man has small penis, looks

over and notices that small man—yay high—has large penis. Yay big. Warlord say, "How is it that small white man like you have so large a penis?" Small man say, "Easy lad. I'm a Leprechaun. I wished it upon myself." Warlord say, "Can you wish one of these upon me?" Leprechaun say, "Sure, lad. But I'd have to have me way wid ya first." Warlord does not like this idea but imagines the many beautiful women that he could have with his new, much larger penis and so he agrees. Warlord bend over. Leprechaun climbs on top and begins business.

"So, what's your name, lad?"
"Abdul."
"Tell me Abdul, what do you do for a living?"
"I am a warlord."
"And how old are you, Abdul?"
"I'm 44."
"Well, Abdul the Warlord, isn't that a bit old to be believin' in Leprechauns?"

ALI ABABWA bursts into hysterics.

ALI ABABWA:

Come on—that's funny! Laugh! Okay. If you didn't like that, you should leave now because it's only going to get worse. I see. No warlords in this audience tonight, no! This is a refined—

Sirens go off. Lights flash. TIM runs around, scared.

Ladies and gentlemen, please do not be alarmed.

The video screen flickers and comes to life. MOHANDES appears on the screen. He is in full security guard garb. A box of Tim Hortons Timbits is displayed prominently in the frame.

MOHANDES:

Attention, theatregoers! Attention, theatregoers! I regret to inform you that the risk of a violent attack has increased considerably since these two gentlemen entered the stage.

ALI HAKIM:

Ali and Ali Security Expert.

ALI ABABWA:

Mr. Zia.

MOHANDES:

No, say my full name. I am Dr. Mohandes Panir Ali Zia Gandhinehrukhomeinijinnah.

ALI HAKIM:

Doctor, what exactly is the level of threat?

MOHANDES:

The level of threat is determined by up-to-date information gathered by me, Dr. Mohandes Panir Ali Zia Gandhinehrukhomeinijinnah.

ALI ABABWA:

Yes yes, we know.

MOHANDES:

These threat assessments are, of course, code-named for maximum clarity. Based on the latest top-secret information, the security threat is now ... Boot Cut.

ALI ABABWA:

Boot Cut?

MOHANDES:

Yes. This level of the Mohandes Panir Threat
Level Assessment System is now proudly brought
to you by the Gap.

ALI HAKIM:

The Gap?

MOHANDES:

The Corporate Relations Adviser seemed most
enthusiastic to nurture relationship with someone
of my accent.

ALI ABABWA:

But doesn't the Gap subcontract to filthy factories
in lawless free trade zones?

MOHANDES:

Don't be cheeky, Bangalore Breath! We are facing a
Boot Cut Risk of Terrorist Attacks!

MOHANDES reveals his security level chart.

As you can see, The Mohandes Panir Security
System includes five levels of security risk: Decaf,
Double Double, Very High, Boot Cut, and
Extremely High. I am now test-marketing a new
sixth threat level.

ALI ABABWA:

But what security level could be higher than
extremely high?

MOHANDES:

I'm thinking: You-and-All-Your-Loved-Ones-Are-
Going-to-Fucking-Die-ANY-FUCKING-MOMENT!
Level. My extensive research proves that people
who are bored are far more likely to commit
terrorist atrocities. This, of course, is why so many
terrorist attacks occur in the theatre. But mine is
not the realm of politics (or aesthetics) my friend. I
am here to provide security, not evaluate the
righteousness of a cause.

ALI HAKIM:

And we are grateful to have you.

MOHANDES:

Yes. Fortunately for you, I have just deployed my
most recent innovative invention, the Dr.
Mohandes Panir Panopticon. Knowledge is Power,
my friends. Be on your guards. Trust no one.
Watch your backs. Eat Timbits. Dr. Mohandes
Panir Ali Zia Gandhinehrukhomeinijinnah, Head
of Ali and Ali Security. Over and out.

ALI HAKIM:

Dr. Mohandes is former employee of Agraba's
Airport Jafar Ali International.

ALI ABABWA:

Head of Security, Domestic Departures, Left-hand
Side Metal Detector.

ALI HAKIM:

We have brought him to protect you from terrorist
attack.

ALI ABABWA:

Not to mention the aXes of Evil—

ALI HAKIM:

Oh please. Do not burden sophisticated Western audience with this superstitious and primitive mumbolo-jumbolo.

ALI ABABWA:

Mumbolo-jumbolo?

ALI HAKIM:

Shut up.

ALI ABABWA:

What about the death of our Korean, Friday Kim Chee? Or the premature and inexplicable death of former U.S. President Ronald Reagan?[2] The signs are everywhere.

ALI HAKIM:

Pah! Peoples, please feel safe. You are completely cared for. Nothing can happen to you as we have sealed all the exits.

ALI ABABWA:

And finally, if anyone is here a doctor, perhaps he or she could look at my bum?

ALI HAKIM:

You donkey, the good people of Real Life Canada do not want to know about your bum.

---

2. Or relevant, topical absurdity. The proposed "Exorcist" theme park in Iraq, for example.

ALI ABABWA:

> Hath not an Agrabanian eyes, organs, senses, dimensions, afflictions, a bum ...?

ALI HAKIM:

> What is wrong with your bum now? Is it gas?

ALI ABABWA:

> I don't know. It hurts. Please, Ali Hakim, take a look.

ALI HAKIM:

> People in Real Life Canada, please small moment.

> *ALI HAKIM takes ALI ABABWA aside.*

> You fool of a Copt, I have told you: do like the Sammis. Use hand and water technique. But you rub and rub and scrape your delicate pink asshole with harsh papers. It is small wonder.

> *Back to the audience.*

> But NOW ... the show. Please, ladies and gentlemen, sit back, relax, and enjoy.

ALI ABABWA & ALI HAKIM:

> Huah!

> *PROJECTION:*
> *Huah: a phrase used by elite Ranger Special Forces in U.S. Army. See* Black Hawk Down.

> *Music: "Gonna Build a Mountain" by Sammy Davis Jr.*

The lights shift to something snazzy. ALI & ALI
briefly "jazz" dance.

ALI ABABWA & ALI HAKIM:
  Shazzam Hassan al-muta!
  Hello People in Real Life Canada!

ALI HAKIM:
  Do Not Be Afraid!

ALI ABABWA:
  And thank you for coming to Vancouver East
  Church Basement.[3]

ALI HAKIM:
  I am Ali Hakim.

ALI ABABWA:
  And I'm not.

ALI ABABWA & ALI HAKIM:
  Here are our papers.

ALI ABABWA:
  We are stateless refugees.

ALI HAKIM:
  From Agraba.

ALI ABABWA:
  You know, Agraba?

---

3. This was a site-specific reference for the Vancouver East Cultural Centre.
In Toronto, at Theatre Passe Muraille, we said: "Thank you for coming to
Theatre Past Its Prime." In Montreal and Edmonton, something else.

ALI HAKIM:

Land of the clamstones, the Sammis, Kreskin's assistant?

ALI ABABWA:

Agronium-rich republic poking into sea of Agraba?

ALI HAKIM:

We are come

ALI ABABWA:

to explain.

ALI HAKIM:

To spread peace and goodwill, win hearts and minds.

ALI ABABWA:

Maybe get married. I am single and in search of wife. Hello ... Hi.

ALI HAKIM:

To build bridges, mend fences.

ALI ABABWA:

Mow lawns?

ALI HAKIM:

Rebuild trust between our peoples.

ALI ABABWA:

Maybe stay a little while?

ALI HAKIM:

You see, we wish nothing more than to be real like you. Prosperous like you. Legal like you. But, as we say in Agraba, the littlest camel does not make the biggest ... how you say ... poo?

ALI ABABWA:

Or most effective refugee application.

ALI HAKIM:

You can dream big but start small. And so with seed money from the United Furniture Warehouse of Nations we are proud to bring to you

ALI ABABWA:

and the people of Mogadishu, Bosnia, the Congo, Liberia, Senegal, Gaza Strip, and South Surrey-White Rock[4]

ALI HAKIM:

our show

ALI ABABWA & ALI HAKIM:

World Dreaming Together. Starring Don—

TIM:

Tom.

ALI ABABWA & ALI HAKIM:

Tim ... Butler!

---

4. Another site-specific reference. In Toronto, we said Rosedale. In Montreal, Verdun-West Island. In Edmonton, Sherwood Park. People love that shtick.

They sing "The World Dreaming Together Song":

From the towers of Calcutta
To the sewers of U.S.A.
To all the men and women
And yes, even the gay
From the old man who lost his nutter
To the child allergic to peanut butter
From the clamstone diver in the sea
To you and you and me

This is the World Dreaming Together Show
We are hoping for a sunny day with lovely weather
throughout the week
A great big chickpea we're baking
To feed the soul of everyone
Do they know it's dreaming together time right now?
Do they know it's dreaming together time right now?

Overcome with emotion, they embrace.

ALI HAKIM:

Pretty good so long, huh?

ALI ABABWA:

You must forgive our English; is not always 100
percent. Fortunately, we have technology. VoxTec
Phraseolator. Very nice. Is "machine translator"
used by Americans to communicate with liberated
civilians in occupied zones.

A demonstration. Let us say we wished to discuss
the complexities of contemporary geo-politics,
perhaps the impact of holding oil reserves in euros

instead of dollars. We simply type in the Agrabanian and ... jumping jinnis, here comes the translation:

ALI HAKIM types. The machine responds.

PHRASEOLATOR (*voice over*):
PUT DOWN THE GOAT!

ALI ABABWA:
You see? Excellent tool for trans-cultural negotiations.

ALI HAKIM:
Tim?!

TIM enters.

Take this away.

He follows TIM off, blaming him for the phraseolator's malfunction.

ALI ABABWA:
Yes, friends, here at Ali and Ali we make every effort to communicate with you in ways to which you are culturally accustomed and so provide many opportunities to purchase merchandise and commemorative memorabilia like *this* ...

PROJECTION:
A commemorative plate.

authentic "Royal Doulton" plate.

Interested in franchise, investment, or sponsorship opportunities? Please check our website—www dot

ALI HAKIM ululates.[5]

dot com. As graduates of the Agrabanian Institute of Niche Marketing, Cross-Polinization, and Higher Colonics, we understand how to synergize our product to extract full value in the post-deal phase.

ALI HAKIM:
But don't worry. We will not be harassing you.

ALI ABABWA:
Or involving you in the show.

A big light shines on a portion of the audience.

ALI HAKIM:
Or shining a big light on you.

ALI ABABWA:
Or singling you out.

ALI HAKIM:
Or in any way embarrassing you like in stupid clown shows.

ALI ABABWA:
NO.

The audience light fades.

---

5. That crazy-ass tongue-wailing Arab types do in moments of emotional intensity.

ALI HAKIM:

Whew. That sure made me hungry. (*to ALI ABABWA*) Did you speak to manager? No? I wish I had a pizza. Oh, pizza. I love pizza. (*to audience*) You like pizza? You do? Great.

He enters the audience and addresses one person in particular.

Give me twenty dollars and we get pizza. Come on. Give me twenty dollars. I thought you said you like pizza. (*he improvises depending on audience response*) How 'bout you put it on gold card. You get points; I get pizza. What, you ate before the show? Must be nice.

He returns to stage.

They think nobody else needs to eat.

ALI ABABWA:

Now before we go any further, any peoples who are with Immigration Department, please please identify yourselves to us after the show; we have special packages for you.

ALI HAKIM:

Nothing big.

ALI ABABWA:

Humble really. Just a way for us to say we really really appreciate anything you can do to keep us from going back to miserable stink hole detention centre in Axerbijan. (*sotto voce*) Ali Hakim!

ALI ABABWA gestures to back of the audience.

Is that him?

ALI HAKIM looks to where ALI ABABWA indicated.

ALI HAKIM:
Oh my Sammi!

Ladies and gentlemen: We are tickled pink to
announce that tonight in the audience we are
blessed with presence of major Canadian media
personality, host of *Canada Now* on CBCNN, and
our hero ...

ALI ABABWA & ALI HAKIM:
Ian Handsomemanthing!

> *They dance lewdly to sexy music.*

> *PROJECTION:*
> *A snazzy promotional photo of Ian Hanomansing.*

> *They ululate and do a brief tribal dance.*

ALI ABABWA:
I knew you would come, Ian!

ALI HAKIM:
Holy hookahs, you are big cheese in Agraba.

ALI ABABWA:
That face. Look at your face. And your skin! Rich
brown nuttiness.

ALI HAKIM:
We are very great admirers of you, Successful
Brown Person, and have a proposition for you!

Perhaps you are looking to make lateral move in world of entertainment, from handsome brown anchor to handsome brown actor?

ALI ABABWA:

We propose a modest proposal of interest to you and all entertainment industry peoples here tonight. We at Ali and Ali have idea for movie vehicle.

ALI HAKIM:

It's an action movie.

ALI ABABWA:

An epic.

ALI HAKIM:

A love story.

ALI ABABWA:

A quiet drama of personal fortitude.

ALI HAKIM:

The movie opens. No credits.

ALI ABABWA:

Some bad motherfuckers come to town, yes?

ALI HAKIM:

Some of the worst motherfuckers.

ALI ABABWA:

They're dirty.

ALI HAKIM:
They have greasy hair.

ALI ABABWA:
Ugly clothes from Wal-Mart.

ALI HAKIM:
They're dark.

ALI ABABWA:
With a dark purpose.

ALI HAKIM:
Swarthy.

ALI ABABWA:
Greasy hair.

ALI HAKIM:
Their underarms are pungent.

ALI ABABWA:
They're religious.

ALI HAKIM:
Fanatics.

ALI ABABWA & ALI HAKIM:
SO.

ALI ABABWA:
They come to town these very bad men.

ALI HAKIM:
Any town.

ALI ABABWA:
Hometown.

ALI HAKIM:
Your town.

ALI ABABWA:
For what purpose we do not yet know.

ALI HAKIM:
We know only they are fanatics.

ALI ABABWA:
Because they are always praying and muttering and looking sideways out of their squinty suspicious eyes with jealousy and envy at the material wealth and FREEDOM the people of Hometown enjoy which the bad men call decadence but secretly LONG FOR. They go to a STRIP BAR.

ALI HAKIM:
Sick disgusting pigs; they do not tip after the lap dance.

ALI ABABWA:
And the next day in a devastating act of criminal monumentality they kill themselves somehow and kill many many tender sweet innocent people who have children or pets or are children or pets themselves.

ALI HAKIM:
Sick.

ALI ABABWA:
People are understandably upset.

ALI HAKIM:
They weep.

ALI ABABWA:
They search for their loved ones among the rubbles.

ALI HAKIM:
Calling out the names. Sally!

ALI ABABWA:
Tercel!

ALI HAKIM:
Atanarjuat!

ALI ABABWA:
They cry out:

ALI HAKIM:
Who has done this?

ALI ABABWA:
Who is responsible?

ALI HAKIM:
Smash cut to

ALI ABABWA:
your boys.

ALI HAKIM:
  Good boys.

ALI ABABWA:
  And some girls too.

ALI HAKIM:
  In they come.

ALI ABABWA:
  They do not want revenge.

ALI HAKIM:
  No. They want justice.

ALI ABABWA:
  They want to liberate people of small dusty
  country that had absolutely nothing to do with the
  unspeakable crime we just saw, a few minutes ago,
  in the movie.

ALI HAKIM:
  They have no quarrel with PEOPLE of small dust
  country.

ALI ABABWA:
  No.

ALI HAKIM:
  Therefore, they kill by the dozens.

ALI ABABWA:
  The hundreds.

ALI HAKIM:

The thousands. Tanks crush houses.

ALI ABABWA:

Dusty brainwashed people rush to defend their city.

ALI HAKIM:

Some of them are burned alive. Or mangled by machine-gun fire.

ALI ABABWA:

In broken-down alleys they fight hand to hand.

ALI HAKIM:

A mouthful of dusty teeth meet the butt of a rifle.

ALI ABABWA:

Gums bleed.

ALI HAKIM:

Eyes pop.

ALI ABABWA & ALI HAKIM:

Women scream.

ALI ABABWA:

The bodies and pieces pile up.

ALI HAKIM:

Here a leg.

ALI ABABWA:

There an arm.

ALI HAKIM:

>   Everywhere a dead man.

ALI ABABWA:

>   And then your boys, surrounded by the dead and
>   dying villagers, call the remaining people of small
>   dusty country together

ALI HAKIM:

>   and your boys give the peoples bottles of water.

ALI ABABWA:

>   And the skies open up and it rains—

ALI HAKIM:

>   think *Black Hawk Down* meets *Singing in the
>   Rain*—

ALI ABABWA:

>   it rains pop tarts!

ALI HAKIM:

>   We push in close to the face of a small dusty old
>   woman.

>   *Poignant violin music sneaks in.*

ALI ABABWA:

>   Her face is worn.

ALI HAKIM:

>   Sorrowful.

ALI ABABWA:
> She looks at the bottle of water in one hand and the pop tart in the other

ALI HAKIM:
> and then at the soldier—

ALI ABABWA:
> this is you, Ian—

ALI HAKIM:
> nicely backlit by the setting sun

ALI ABABWA:
> and her eyes fill with tears

ALI HAKIM:
> of thankfulness,

ALI ABABWA:
> of wonder.

ALI HAKIM:
> She understands.

ALI ABABWA:
> This is no ordinary war. These are not soldiers such as they know from before.
>
> Act 2: In the city there is a boy, Ali.

ALI HAKIM:
> He cares nothing for politics or this or that.

ALI ABABWA:

No.

ALI HAKIM:

He cares only for football.

ALI ABABWA:

Soccer, as you say.

ALI HAKIM:

This boy plays in the dusty alleys with other boys using a ball made of rags from his older brothers' shirts.

ALI ABABWA:

But this boy, playing soccer, does not notice

ALI HAKIM:

the anti-personnel land mine

ALI ABABWA:

that has been left behind by your boys—

ALI HAKIM:

good boys!—

ALI ABABWA:

and so on.

ALI HAKIM:

Ali loses his legs and arms and some of his face and—

ALI ABABWA:

Enough! Ali lies in a hospital bed.

ALI HAKIM:

He has an indomitable spirit.

ALI ABABWA:

And your boys are beside themselves when they find out what has happened to Ali for they used to watch him playing with his friends and marvel at his speed and grace and agility. They go to see Ali in the hospital. One of your boys weeps—

ALI HAKIM:

this is you, Ian—

ALI ABABWA:

"This damned war."

ALI HAKIM:

But Ali is not angry. He is peaceful.

ALI ABABWA:

For he has seen how your boys have already transformed his country; how his friends, the urchins of the streets, are happier, even though their schools are destroyed and they have no running water and their parents are being sexually tortured in the prisons of the former dictator.

ALI HAKIM:

As Ali lies in his hospital cot he speaks of soccer and his hero, the great English metrosexual soccer player, David Bendham, and how he dreamed of one day playing against Bendham and, of course, losing but that would be okay because after the

game he would trade shirts with Bendham, having
won his respect having played so valiantly.

ALI ABABWA:
SO,

ALI HAKIM:
your boys climb in a jeep

ALI ABABWA:
and set off hundreds of kilometres

ALI HAKIM:
across dangerous territory

ALI ABABWA:
where surely they will encounter pockets of fierce
resistance

ALI HAKIM:
to find the British soldiers.

ALI ABABWA:
And when the British soldiers hear the story of Ali
they give your boys Bendham's shirt.

ALI HAKIM:
And when your boys set off again

ALI ABABWA:
one of the Brits is heard to say,

ALI HAKIM:
into the darkness of the desert night,

ALI ABABWA:

"This damned war."

ALI HAKIM:

Back in our jeep there is silence.

ALI ABABWA:

The sort of silence you get when it's dark and men drive a jeep through hostile territory to deliver a soccer shirt to a boy with no arms. Suddenly

ALI HAKIM:

an ambush.

ALI ABABWA:

Incoming RPG!

ALI HAKIM:

The jeep explodes in a fireball of fire.

ALI ABABWA:

Your boys rush out of the jeep, weapons at the ready.

ALI HAKIM:

And then they realize:

ALI ABABWA:

the soccer shirt.

ALI HAKIM:

It's still in the flaming jeep.

ALI ABABWA:

And meanwhile the enemy is advancing.

ALI HAKIM:
Scary gibberish music plays.

Scary gibberish music plays.

ALI ABABWA:
One of your boys plunges into the maelstrom that is the flaming jeep—

ALI HAKIM:
this is you, Ian—

ALI ABABWA:
while the others keep the enemy at bay.

ALI HAKIM:
They're outnumbered

ALI ABABWA:
but they fight on.

ALI HAKIM:
For Ali.

ALI ABABWA:
For Bendham.

ALI HAKIM:
For transcendence.

ALI ABABWA:
For reasons of personal integrity we may never understand.

ALI HAKIM:
And they hear you call,

ALI ABABWA:
"I've got the shirt!" And it's untouched.

ALI HAKIM:
It had been under a flameproof something or other.

ALI ABABWA:
And in your excitement you wave the shirt

ALI HAKIM:
and the enemy sees the movement

ALI ABABWA:
and—

A loud gun shot.

ALI HAKIM:
A single shot splits the still desert night.

ALI ABABWA:
And you fall.

ALI HAKIM:
Still clutching the shirt.

ALI ABABWA:
Your friends rush to you

ALI HAKIM:
but you say,

ALI ABABWA:

"Take the shirt. Get it to Ali, I'll hold them off, get out of here, go!"

ALI HAKIM:

But the leader of the group—

ALI ABABWA:

this is perhaps Paul Gross—

ALI HAKIM:

says, "None of my boys get left behind."

ALI ABABWA:

And forming a crude stretcher out of bits of the jeep

ALI HAKIM:

they put you, Ian, on it

ALI ABABWA:

and go berserk.

They ululate.

ALI HAKIM:

Except in English.

ALI ABABWA:

Charging in slow motion, the shells expelled from their guns in a languid and glorious balletic choreography.

ALI HAKIM:

And the enemy is overwhelmed

ALI ABABWA:

even though the boys are in slow motion.

ALI HAKIM:

Your boys

ALI ABABWA:

good boys

ALI HAKIM:

the best boys

ALI ABABWA:

jog the hundreds of remaining kilometres back to the city

ALI HAKIM:

carrying you on the stretcher

ALI ABABWA:

back to the hospital where they left Ali.

ALI HAKIM:

They made a promise after all.

ALI ABABWA:

But when they get there Ali is dead already.

ALI HAKIM:

The pretty brown nurse in the starched white uniform with the button missing here and the shapely legs and the pillowy—

ALI ABABWA:

Salma Hayek perhaps—

ALI HAKIM:

> she says Ali died happy knowing they'd bring the shirt only he couldn't wait that long, they needed him in heaven to play soccer, and she cries, falling into your manly arms, Ian.

ALI ABABWA:

> You are healing quickly.

ALI HAKIM:

> And the boys their faces are hard.

ALI ABABWA:

> The things they've seen.

ALI HAKIM:

> The prices they've paid.

ALI ABABWA:

> And it's too much for one of them and he tears off his Special Forces shirt and puts on the soccer jersey crying out, "I am Ali!"

ALI HAKIM:

> This is you, Ian!

ALI ABABWA:

> You feel a special bond with the young Ali.

ALI HAKIM:

> And crazed with grief and sorrow you rush into a machine-gun nest and with your bare brown hands you tear it apart. The enemy attacks you but you squish them like so many mosquitoes.

ALI ABABWA:

> In a moment of great heroism and poignancy you pass from this world to the next. You are transcendent. You fulfill your destiny.

ALI HAKIM:

> Back at the base

ALI ABABWA:

> it is Asian Heritage Night and the soft sounds of a Hawaiian luau drift into the tent where the rest of the company sits in a circle.

> *We hear the soft sounds of Hawaiian luau music.*

ALI HAKIM:

> They are solemn now, slouched against their cots.

ALI ABABWA:

> Some smoke, some stare numbly at their hands but it is you, Ian, that they think of, their fallen comrade: the one who dared to die for something a little bit more ...

ALI HAKIM:

> And as we pull back from the tent up high into the air, the hot desert wind blows, whipping the tattered remains of a child's soccer jersey up from the dusty street, up above the prefabricated tents, up past Old Glory herself, but in the distance we hear the thin wail of the muezzin

> *From off we hear the muezzin call in gibberish.*

> calling the faithful to prayer.

We hear the muezzin sing "Kill all the white guys."

The End.

ALI ABABWA:

I think I smell an Oscar.

ALI HAKIM:

Do you?

Enter DUNCAN.

DUNCAN:

Excuse me. Can I have some light here? *(he addresses the audience)* I apologize for the interruption, ladies and gentlemen.

ALI ABABWA & ALI HAKIM:

Theatre's manager!

DUNCAN:

My name is Duncan McVingoe and I'm the Artistic and Managing Producer here at the Vancouver East Cultural Centre. And first, I'd like to thank everyone for coming. Thank you. It's an honour to have you. Welcome. I'd also like to make it clear that our mandate to represent, accommodate, dignify, and empower cultural communities through theatrical productions of high artistic quality doesn't mean that—well ...

ALI HAKIM:

Ask him.

ALI ABABWA:
You.

DUNCAN:
Well, it means we have a responsibility to you, our
audience, a responsibility we tek seriously, which is
why I've taken the extraordinary step of interruptin'
and ... Excuse us please. Excuse me.

He turns to ALI & ALI.

ALI ABABWA & ALI HAKIM:
Mr. Manager! Salaam aleikum.

DUNCAN:
Could we speak ah privately fer a moment?

ALI ABABWA & ALI HAKIM:
Sure.

*They step upstage. In a furious whisper DUNCAN
berates ALI & ALI.*

DUNCAN:
Right then.

Ladies and gentlemen, again I apologize for the
unorthodox interruption. However, as part of our
pro-active education and outreach mandate, I feel
it is necessary to facilitate ongoing dialogue for
personal and intercultural exploration.

ALI & ALI nod vigorously and give thumbs-up.[6]

---

6. Though in some parts of the Middle East, the "thumbs-up" gesture is
rude, Ali and Ali are conversant with North American idioms.

Ye see, we had agreed that they would present a new ethnic family drama. Hadn't we?

More vigorous agreement from ALI & ALI.

After all, that's what ye came to see—an ethnic family drama that offers you a window onto our nation's cultural diversity yet resonates with universal themes. So tha's what they're goin' to be doin' now ... *(with a significant glance at ALI & ALI)* Right?

ALI ABABWA:
Mr. Manager, small moment before we—

DUNCAN:
Right?

ALI ABABWA:
Right.

DUNCAN:
Back to our show, ladies and gentlemen.

ALI ABABWA & ALI HAKIM:
Huah!

ALI & ALI prepare the stage.

ALI ABABWA:
(to audience) Apologies. The esteemed Manager is, of course, correct. We agreed to present to you a manycultural peoples' ancestral drama, which we will do in due course. It is just, you know, with you

and us all in the same room, together, we get excited and make mischief.

VOICE OVER:

Ladies and girls, boys and men, Ali and Ali proudly present a new Canadian play: *Grasshopper White Eyes Dreams of Home.*

TIM enters, wearing a coolie hat with authentic pigtail sown into it, an apron, and carrying a butcher knife. He plays DAD. ALI HAKIM plays CHARLIE.

DAD:

Son, I understand you're feeling conflicted.

CHARLIE:

You understand? You understand??!! Did you go to school in an all-white neighbourhood when you were growing up in Dao Dong Long province? Did you have to endure bad jokes about the shape of your eyes, the colour of your skin, or your bad driving habits? Did you have kids in your cafeteria puking their guts out just because you had a chicken claw snack pack?

You understand? You understand? Do you understand what it feels like to feel like a fruit—a banana—yellow on the outside but white on the inside?

He moves to the window special.

Do you feel your soul ripping to pieces because there are two people battling inside of you? A battle that cannot be won because one side is screaming with passion: I am Charlie Chew! I like pitch and putt. And the other side is screaming with equal passion: I am Chew Mao Dong Hung! Grasshopper Stands Firm Against Foreign Devil Oppressor!

Do you understand that I am burning in the flames of internalized racism? Fuck your understanding. I'm tired of seeing the world through white eyes! I'm a chink and I'm proud! Fuck you Daddy! Fuck you! I hate you! I hate you! I hate you Daddy!!

DAD:
Son, I love you no matter wha'.

CHARLIE breaks down into his father's arms, crying.

CHARLIE:
I love you, Daddy. I love you. I love you. I'm Canadian dammit. I'm Canadian.

DAD:
There there, we're all Canadian, Charlie. We're all Canadian.

Moving to embrace CHARLIE, DAD accidentally impales his son with the butcher knife.

CHARLIE:
Daddy?

DAD:
Charlie?

CHARLIE dies. DAD moves to the window special.

DAD:

Damn you, Canadian Dream!

Weeping, DAD commits seppuku,[7] carving a maple leaf into his belly. ALI ABABWA applauds. Actors leap up and take a bow.

ALI ABABWA:

Wasn't that wonderful? Ladies and sons, please remember that here at Ali and Ali we have a fine selection of wide merchandise available for purchase. Remember at the top of show when Ali Hakim said

TIM:

"Aren't you a little old to be believing in Leprechauns?"

ALI ABABWA:

Why not remember that moment forever, with a commemorative Ali and Ali Irish Culture Pillowcase? Only $24.99 for a full set.

PROJECTION:
Pillowcase set with a depraved-looking Leprechaun on it.

ALI ABABWA:

Or a

TIM ululates (lebulebulebu!).

Mug.

7. Ritual suicide by disembowelment formerly practiced by Japanese samurai. Also called hara-kiri. Look it up.

PROJECTION:
A coffee mug with "Lebulebulebulebu" embossed on it.

ALI ABABWA:
It's like

TIM does Homer Simpson.

TIM:
D'oh!

ALI ABABWA:
but better.

Or perhaps some of you are Middle East history buffs? Remember when Jafar Ali Salim led the Agrabanian General Strike of 1968? This pivotal moment in Middle East History is commemorated forever in this bauxite miniature lovingly handcrafted by fairly-compensated wood elves from the Brown Forest.

PROJECTION:
Miniature of General Strike.

It can be yours for only $99.99 of your pretty Canadian dollars.

Pause.

No? That's OK, we can haggle. We're a haggling people. $17.99. And I'll throw in the commemorative strikebreakers. Hoo, you're good. Drive hard bargain. No accident Western world is on top, huh? $12.99. I pick up GST. God, you're killing me here.

ALI HAKIM:

> (*storming back on*) How about 5 bucks for a meatball sandwich?

ALI ABABWA:

> Calm down, Ali Hakim. Is OK. Is free market. Too bad you don't want to buy because tonight only we are going to donate one percent of every purchase to Agraba City Fire Department. Perhaps you don't know about Agraba City Fire Department. They are very short on equipment. You know, like infrared sensors, breathing apparatus, engines, hoses, ladders, a pole. Water.

ALI HAKIM:

> Stop. That's enough, all this bullshit. There's no fire department in Agraba. Provisional Authority disbanded fire department. For being part of old regime. Only fire department I will give money to is the one making fire in occupiers' tanks.

ALI ABABWA:

> (*laughs exaggeratedly*) Oh. Ali Hakim is having the irony. My friends, there is great need for modern fire department in Agraba today, to put out all the explosions. If you buy pillowcase we give you Agraba City Fire Department decal for proud display in Hummer. Come on.

ALI HAKIM:

> Cheap bastards. You Canadians—you can't buy me a slice of pizza? How much did you make selling weapons to Americans, huh? Who armed the fundamentalists!

ALI ABABWA:

> You mean the Zionists? 'Cause they're still arming the Zionists.

ALI HAKIM:

> No, I mean the Other Fundamentalists! (*he speaks in Agrabanian*) Our fundamentalists!

ALI ABABWA:

> Ali Hakim. They do not speak your language.

ALI HAKIM:

> My language? (*pause*)
>
> *ALI HAKIM turns to the audience.*
>
> They have done this to us. Long live the Revolutionary Front for the Liberation of Agraba. And fuck you!

ALI ABABWA:

> Ali Hakim. No no no. TIM!

ALI HAKIM:

> Fuck all you in your peaceful West. Oh sure, you think I am violent and disrespectful, huh? Why don't I embrace your fucking democracy? I wonder?! 100 years ago you called it civilization, and you're still shoving it down our throats!
>
> *TIM runs on and tranquilizes ALI HAKIM with a needle in the neck. ALI HAKIM instantly collapses. TIM drags him off to a corner and revives him.*

ALI ABABWA:

My friends, please. Ali Hakim is very—aroused?
He has much on his serving dish, many worries,
responsibilities. But let us not let that trouble us
now. Hey! Please, good peoples, take your time
choosing what is right for you and your lifestyle.
You may at any time during the show signal your
interest in buying something simply by calling out,
"Hey, I'd like to buy that pillowcase," or these
shirts that we are wearing or that life-like civet cat
featured in *Grasshopper White Eyes Dreams of
Home*. Whatever you desire. We are—due to
circumstances beyond our control—practicing neo-
liberals, and will sell pretty much anything for a
price.

ALI HAKIM is successfully revived by TIM.

ALI HAKIM:

Oh, I had the most beautiful dream. I was with my
Ana in Agra—(*he sees TIM and the audience*) (*to
TIM*) What are you doing, fool? Go bring the goods
for Ababwa to sell to good people of Real Life
Canada. (*he kicks TIM; turns to ALI ABABWA*)
What?

ALI ABABWA:

They're not buying.

ALI HAKIM:

Nothing?

ALI ABABWA:

They don't like us.

ALI HAKIM:
Why? What did you do?

ALI ABABWA:
Me?

ALI ABABWA shakes his head.

ALI HAKIM:
They look frightened. Are you frightened? Did Ali
Ababwa make intestinal wind? Ask you to examine
his bum? I am sorry.

ALI ABABWA:
It is you, Ali Hakim. You are so aggressive.

ALI HAKIM:
When?

No no! Ali Ababwa, you indigenous monkey—of
course! It is because you are blue![8] *(turning to
audience)* It is off-putting, no? *(back to ALI
ABABWA)* We must explain. They know nothing of
the Sammites and the Copts.

ALI ABABWA:
I don't know.

ALI HAKIM:
For sure. It's important that they understand.
Context is everything. *(he addresses the audience)*
Agraba is a predominantly Muslim society.

8. Ali Ababwa's face—or a good part of it—is blue. See Disney's *Aladdin.*

ALI ABABWA:
Not Shia.

ALI HAKIM:
Not Sunni.

ALI ABABWA:
But Sammi.

ALI HAKIM:
As you know, the Shia Muslim believe that at some point there will appear in the world a 12th Imam to carry on the work of the Prophet Mohammed, peace be upon him.

ALI ABABWA:
The Sunnis believe something else.

ALI HAKIM:
The Sammis, on the other case, believe that there is a 13th Imam who has already appeared.

ALI ABABWA:
In Vegas.

ALI HAKIM:
He has come to Earth and assumed the form of a dynamic

ALI ABABWA:
one-eyed

ALI HAKIM:
black

ALI ABABWA:
Jewish

ALI HAKIM:
entertainer

ALI ABABWA:
named

ALI HAKIM:
Sammy.

ALI ABABWA:
Davis Junior.

> *A burst of "Gonna Build a Mountain" by Sammy Davis Jr. plays.*

ALI HAKIM:
Sammis are the eponymous followers of Sammy Davis.

ALI ABABWA:
Eponymous?

ALI HAKIM:
Yes, you know it means ...

PHRASEOLATOR (*voice over*):
PUT DOWN THE GOAT!

> *ALI HAKIM glares offstage and hisses at TIM to turn the phraseolator off.*

ALI ABABWA:

The holy book of the Sammis is the Bojang, which interprets many of the lyrics of Sammy Davis's best songs. I've never actually read it but ...

ALI HAKIM:

It is full of good advice.

ALI ABABWA:

Be good. Share and co-operate.

ALI HAKIM:

Use your words not your fists.

ALI ABABWA:

Talk to animals.

ALI HAKIM:

It is a religion of moderation, kindness, tolerance ... and martinis.

ALI ABABWA:

But in Agraba there is a group of fanatical Sammis.

ALI HAKIM:

A *small* group. Fundamentalists. Known as Sammites, they poke out their left eyes and, in the throes of religious ecstasy, tap dance until their feet are mere bloody stumps. Years ago with the aid of the U.S., the Sammites gained control of Agraba and imposed a theocratic state. In addition to reducing the legal status of women to that of camels they began sweeping oppression of

Agraba's minority Christians, an ancient sect
known as the Copts.

ALI ABABWA:

COPTS. Not cops. Cop-t-s. There's a *t.* (*he indicates*
the projection)

PROJECTION:
Copt/kopt/ n.
a Christian of the Coptic Church.
[French Copte from Modern Latin Coptus from
Arabic al-kibt, al-kubt]

PROJECTION:
Coptic Church n.
of the Jacobite sect upholding the Monophysite
Doctrine, condemned by the Council of Chalcedon;
for eleven centuries have had possession of the
patriarchal chair of Alexandria.

ALI ABABWA:

In an orgy of violence known to us as Coptellnacht,
the Sammite religious police desecrated our
temples, scattered our icons, and poisoned our
Pope. Agraba's few Copts were hunted down and
our faces were dipped in vats of blue dye to signify
our outsider status.

ALI HAKIM:

Once again, Ali Ababwa, on behalf of all Sammis, I
am truly sorry.

ALI ABABWA
I know.

Still, my friends, you must not underestimate us. Despite hailing from a country hijacked by an oppressive theocratic regime, Agrabanians are well-educated and forward-thinking people, poised to take advantage of a growing and dynamic global economy. We are here, and available to work in many capacities.

ALI HAKIM looks at ALI ABABWA curiously; ALI ABABWA makes reassuring noises and presses on with his pitch.

We have very impressive and wide range of employment experience. For example, as event caterers, when Rumsfeld met Saddam in Baghdad.

PROJECTION:
Photo of Donald Rumsfeld's visit to Baghdad when Saddam was still a buddy, with ALI HAKIM inserted in the background.

ALI HAKIM:
But we are not available for employment here as we must return to Agraba as soon as—

ALI ABABWA:
(*intently studying the photograph*) One moment, Ali Hakim, what is this in picture ...?

ALI HAKIM:
What?

ALI ABABWA:
This shadow. It was not in original image.

ALI HAKIM:

TIM! Prepare the enhancer.

He exits.

ALI ABABWA:

Scan northwest 27,000 degrees. Zoom. Give me
50 percent. 10 more. Enhance.

*With each instruction, the image changes until
some words can be dimly discerned. Finally, the
message becomes clear: THE DARK AXES ARE
COMING!*

Oh my God Oh my God Ali Hakim, ALI HAKIM—

ALI HAKIM:

(*re-entering*) What, Ali Ababwa?

ALI ABABWA:

The Dark aXes are coming! It said so in the picture.
The Dark aXes of el Mutah. The aXes of Mass
Destruction.

ALI HAKIM:

Holy Hummus, Ali Ababwa! On picture—is
nothing—just shadow of moon on lens.

ALI ABABWA:

What did you say? Shadow of Moon?!

ALI HAKIM:

So?

ALI ABABWA:
You know the prophesy as well as I.

He recites.

"I'm being followed by a moonshadow
Moonshadow moonshadow
Leaping and hopping on a moonshadow
Moonshadow, moonshadow."

ALI HAKIM:
Oh my Sammi! You are right! I am shitting
myself! What should we do?

ALI ABABWA:
TIM! BRING THE BIG BUTTON!

TIM runs out with the security alert button.

ALI ABABWA & ALI HAKIM:
Shazaaaaam!

*They press the button. ALI HAKIM kicks TIM off the
stage. The screen flickers to life. MOHANDES is
eating a donut and reading Bob Woodward's* Bush
at War. *Behind him, an image of a bikini babe is
on his computer screen.*

MOHANDES:
This is Mohandes Panir Ali Zia ... One moment
please.

He swallows the remains of the donut.

Gandhinehrukhomeinijinnah. Have you caught a
terrorist?

ALI ABABWA:

We have an important mission for you.

MOHANDES:

What are you talking about, Madras Man? I am
very busy profiling potential terrorist suspects.

*MOHANDES looks back to his computer screen and
attempts to shut it off.*

ALI ABABWA:

You must increase the security threat assessment!

MOHANDES:

Don't tell me what the level of threat should be. I am
Mohandes Panir Ali Zia Gandhinehrukhomeinijinnah!
The absence of evidence does not necessarily
indicate the evidence of absence.

ALI ABABWA:

Shut up! The Evil aXes have been deployed. You
must find them. The fate of the world hangs in the
balance.

MOHANDES:

Evil aXes? Oh, yes. My intelligence sources have
indicated that these aXes of Evil would be used.
These terrorists are very wily. They will stop at
nothing. They are within my grasp. I will find
them!

MOHANDES gets up and exits the frame.

(*from off-screen*) Hey Bindi! You want double double
from Tim Hortons?

ALI ABABWA:

OK, now, back to show.

ALI HAKIM:

Ladies and gentlemen, we are proud to bring to you one of our country's beautiful artistic traditions: The Classical Puppet Theatre of Agraba.

With TIM, they assume their positions at the puppet theatre. The "puppets" are photocopied faces of George W. Bush, Dick Cheney, Donald Rumsfeld, and Colin Powell, on sticks, against a background photo of the Oval Office. The puppet show is projected onto the screen by a live camera.

DUBYA:

OK, so what's on the agenda?

CHENEY:

Mr. President, we need to discuss the report.

DUBYA:

Oh yeah. (*pause*) Which report?

CHENEY:

The Comprehensive Analysis of Challenges in the Occupation of Iraq report.

DUBYA:

Oh yeah. What's it about?

CHENEY:

It's about the challenges in the occupation of Iraq.

DUBYA:

Right. Did you read it, Rummy?

RUMMY:

It's bullshit.

DUBYA:

Summarize it for me, would you Dick?

CHENEY:

Mr. President, it's seventeen volumes of densely—

DUBYA:

Try, Dick.

CHENEY:

Well, basically, sir, it says that given ideal conditions we could be successful in Iraq.

DUBYA:

I like that.

RUMMY:

I love it.

DUBYA:

Me too, I love it too actually.

SEMI-COLIN:

(*entering*) Hey are you guys having a meeting without me?

RUMMY:

Irie, man.

DUBYA:

Oh hi, Semi-Colin.

RUMMY:

'Sup dog?

SEMI-COLIN:

Mr. President, the media are having a field day
with the prison abuse—

RUMMY:

Fuck 'em. Keeps their mind off the really nasty shit
we're doing. Hehehe.

DUBYA:

I saw those Abu Gayrab pictures. Didn't I?

CHENEY:

You did, sir.

DUBYA:

Can I see them again?

RUMMY:

No, sir.

CHENEY:

I want to know what kind of fairy-tale world people
are living in. So our boys piled a bunch of naked
guys together—

RUMMY:

Or made some guy wear some woman's
underwear—

CHENEY:

Or made some guys jerk off in public—

RUMMY:

Or jammed a light up some guy's ass—

CHENEY:

I mean, what do they expect?

RUMMY:

Yeah!

CHENEY:

Hell, I look at way better stuff than that on the internet all the time.

RUMMY:

Amen, Fatty!

CHENEY:

Like Rush Limbaugh said, "These soldiers were just blowing off a little steam."

RUMMY:

Flush is a good guy.

CHENEY:

I like him.

RUMMY:

Me too. We should have him over.

CHENEY:

Let him know we appreciate what he does.

RUMMY:

Thank him.

CHENEY:

I'd like to shake his hand.

RUMMY:

I'd give him a pat on the back.

CHENEY:

I'd like to pinch his ass.

RUMMY:

Put a clamp on his balls.

CHENEY:

Let him suck my dick.

RUMMY:

While Semi gives it to his old lady from behind.

CHENEY:

And we watch!

DUBYA:

Oh, just like those frat parties we used to go to.

CHENEY:

That's right, sir.

SEMI-COLIN:

Mr. President, this tort—uh, abuse—

DUBYA:

Semi? You ever talk to God?

SEMI-COLIN:

Uh ... uh ... uh ...

DUBYA:

Dick?

CHENEY:

Not face to face.

DUBYA:

Rummy?

RUMMY:

Oh yeah. We go *way* back.

DUBYA:

Laura and I give thanks to Him for clearing up my haemorrhoids.

Murmurs of congratulations.

You know what He told me last night?

CHENEY:

What, sir?

DUBYA:

He told me that Freedom is His gift to every man and woman in this world. And He said that as the greatest power on the face of the earth we have an obligation to help the spread of freedom.

Agreement.

He told me that the coming apocalypse in the Middle East will herald the beginning of the Second

Coming. He said, there would be peace in the valley and the Jews could be converted to Christianity. And Jesus is gonna sleep over in the Lincoln Bedroom. What do you say to that?

I say let's get to it.

SEMI-COLIN:
To what, Mr. President?

DUBYA:
To spread freedom, we should ...

> *RUMMY whispers the answers to DUBYA one phrase at a time; DUBYA repeats what he has been told.*

Enslave Palestinians in the West Bank ... bankroll some dictators ... give more tax breaks to our really rich friends ... oh yeah, no bugging the Russians about Chechnya and ...

RUMMY:
and put more black guys in jail!

DUBYA:
That's it.

RUMMY:
No offence, Leroy.

DUBYA:
Why would he take offence? Semi's not black.

SEMI-COLIN:
Mr. President uh, I'm uh African-American.

DUBYA:

You see?

SEMI-COLIN:

Mr. President, I don't think those are the sort of measures your father would have approved of.

RUMMY:

His father worked for the CIA! He was an establishment pussy. Fucking weenie.

DUBYA:

Yeah. So, I been thinking.

Murmurs of congratulations.

Listen to this you guys. In the War on Terror, retreat is not an onion.

RUMMY:

Option.

DUBYA:

Ah, I was gonna say that! I was gonna say option but then at the last minute I ... I didn't.

CHENEY:

I wish I had seven cheeseburgers.

He leaves the office, presumably to get seven cheeseburgers.

DUBYA:

Semi-Colin?

SEMI-COLIN:

   Sir.

DUBYA:

   I want a report on that whole apocalypse in the
   Middle East, Second Coming, Jesus returning to
   the Holy Land thing. I want it on my desk by noon
   tomorrow and I want it now!

SEMI-COLIN:

   Sheeeit, what up, dog? Sho, stick it to de negro. I
   ain't no mothafuckin' office boy. I'n de
   mothafuckin' secretary of the mothafuckin' state.
   I'n take dat report and shove it up yo skinny white
   ass, mothafucka. And Rumsfeld, you muthafuckin'
   cracker, any more lip from you and I'n fuck you
   up, mothafucka. (*beat*) I mean, I'll get my people
   on it, sir. Right away.

DUBYA:

   Good.

     As SEMI-COLIN exits, we hear ...

SEMI-COLIN:

   Yo! Condoleezza, get your ass over here, girl!

DUBYA:

   Let me make it very clear. The War on Terror is not
   a figure of speech. It's more like a bumper sticker.

RUMMY:

   Mr. President, let us pray.

     Music: "Ride of the Valkyries" bursts on.

A dart appears stage left in the puppet theatre and impales itself in RUMMY'S head. The music stops.

Is that all you got, ya infidels? Bring it on, camel jockeys!

He begins to sing.

Sharif don't like it!
Rock the casbah!
Rock the casbah!

He stops. Sniffs.

Hey, I wonder if Hillary sat on this desk.

Music: Taraf De Haidouks.

PROJECTION:
Which country alone in the Middle East has nuclear weapons?

Which country in the Middle East refuses to sign the Nuclear Non-Proliferation Treaty and bars international inspectors?

Which country in the Middle East is in defiance of 69 United Nations Security Council resolutions and has been protected from 29 more by U.S. vetoes?

Hint: It's not Agraba.

DUNCAN:
Hang on, hang on.

ALI ABABWA:
Oh, theatre's manager has returned.

DUNCAN:

What was tha'? Look, leave Israel out of it.

ALI HAKIM:

But is it not true?

DUNCAN:

Look, this is not the place, and I'm sure you
(*audience*) agree with me, NAE the place for your
local, petty, feudal grievances, yer decontextualized
finger pointing. The theatre is where we explore the
timeless verities of the human condition. Ladies
and gentlemen, I apologize once again. I turn my
back for a few minutes to get a falafel and—

ALI HAKIM:

Falafel? Did you finish it?

DUNCAN:

This, of course, is part of the challenge of doing
inter-cultural work and we know that ye support
the work we're doing here and we thank ye and
want ye to know that we are constantly striving to
improve.

> *Behind DUNCAN, ALI & ALI hold a heated
> discussion.*

And I'm sure we'll be right back on track
momentarily. (*to ALI & ALI*) So, where's that play ye
started?

ALI HAKIM:

Uh play?

DUNCAN:

The one specified in the contract, remember?!

ALI HAKIM:

Ah, yes, the contract ...

ALI ABABWA:

Entertaining you should mention the contract, because we—

DUNCAN:

So let's get back to it shall we? The father and the boy and the ... Ladies and gentlemen, again I apologize for the interruption but isn't this wha' makes the theatre so special? It's live. Anything can happen. Though usually—and preferably—not with such frequency.

DUNCAN leaves.

ALI HAKIM:

Why didn't you say something?

ALI ABABWA:

Why didn't you? Why must it always be me who does the saying?

ALI HAKIM:

You? *(in Agrabanian)* I always have to get the money.

ALI ABABWA:

No, Ali Hakim. I tell you. Here I am speaking the English.

ALI HAKIM:

Pah! I am always attaining the money. Who made warlord certify cheque in Congo?

ALI ABABWA:

Who pawned watch to bury Friday Kim Chee?

ALI HAKIM:

Who bribed the guards in camp in Axerbijan? And who bought passports to get out of Jerkiistan?

ALI ABABWA:

(*remembering audience*) Ali Hakim ... little camels have big ears ...

ALI HAKIM:

Them?—pah! They don't know what's going on. They think this is part of show.

ALI ABABWA:

Arguing this way will not help us obtain money we are owed from manager.

ALI HAKIM:

Call Tim.

ALI ABABWA:

Tim?

ALI HAKIM:

He wants to be pay, he can speak to manager. Besides, they are same tribe.

ALI ABABWA:

> We must speak to manager. Tim is our hireling.
> He must never know our financial insecurity.

DUNCAN:

> (*from off*) We're still waiting ...

> *ALI & ALI scramble.*

VOICE OVER:

> Ladies and gentlemen, Ali and Ali extremely dearly
> proudly present a new Canadian play: *A Day in the*
> *Life of Ivan Scarberia* or *The Gulag East Etobicoke.*

> *DAD (TIM) slurps borscht. VLADIMIR, his son*
> *(ALI ABABWA) watches in disgust.*

VLADIMIR:

> Dad, I want to talk to you.

DAD:

> Vladimir, eat first, then talk.

VLADIMIR:

> No, Dad, I have something to say. I will not be
> silenced. This is a democracy we live in here, not a
> communist dictatorship. Right? That's why you left
> and came here isn't it? Isn't it?

DAD:

> Eat your borscht.

VLADIMIR:

> You're a gangster. You kill people. You trade in
> small armaments and enslave poor Siberian girls

in local strip clubs. I'm not eating that borscht, Dad. I won't be a part of it anymore. Fuck you Daddy! Fuck you! I hate you! I hate you! I hate you Daddy!!

DAD moves to window special.

DAD:
What do you know, Vladimir? Did you come to new country with only shirt on your back? Did you build home for your family with only two hands and an old Soviet army pistol? You're a pussy, Vladimir. (*he cruelly strikes his son, though the timing of the stage hit is off*) You're soft. (*he strikes him cruelly again*) If we were in Mother Russia I'd shoot you in the head. (*he puts pistol to VLADIMIR'S head, cruelly*)

VLADIMIR:
But we're not in Mother Russia, Daddy.

VLADIMIR punches his father, who catches and crushes VLADIMIR'S fist.

Is that the only tool you have for expressing tenderness and affection towards me?

DAD crushes his fist some more.

Go ahead Dad, crush every bone in my body.

And more.

Can't you see that I am drowning in a tidal wave of Old World, neo-Stalinist, patrio-masculinist repression?

Stung by the truth, DAD releases VLADIMIR.

DAD:

You are right Vladimir. Now I see. I love you, Vladimir.

VLADIMIR:

I love you too, Daddy. I'm Canadian, dammit. I'm Canadian.

DAD:

There, there Vladimir, don't cry. We're all Canadian. We are all Canadian. Come. *(they move to the window special)* I take you to club. It's time for you to meet your mother.

VLADIMIR:

Mother?

> *DAD walks VLADIMIR offstage. He trips and accidentally shoots VLADIMIR.*

DAD:

(off) Vladimi-i-i-i-ir! Damn you, Canadian Dream!

> *Another gunshot.*

> PROJECTION:
> *Blood splatter in the shape of a maple leaf.*

ALI HAKIM:

Bravo, Ali Ababwa! *(indicating to ALI ABABWA that the manager is off in the wings)* Now, we must do scene 3 of ... ethnic peoples manyculture play ...

ALI ABABWA:

Ah yes, scene 3. It is called ... *Jimmy Two Feathers Runs with Pizza Box* or (*he makes Native American ululation sound*)[9] *West Edmonton Mall.*

They set the scene again. DUNCAN enters while they set up and stands upstage, arms crossed, regarding them sceptically. ALI & ALI see him and give an enthusiastic thumbs-up. ALI ABABWA plays DAD; ALI HAKIM plays JOHNNY. DAD pretends to chop something on the tabletop. His chopping becomes a rhythmic drumming pattern. He begins to "sing" Native-style.

DAD:

HihowareyaareyaareyaHihowareyaareyaareya Hihowareya. Son, where's my smokes?

JOHNNY:

You understand?

DUNCAN:

Oh come on! What do ye take me for? They're all the same, those scenes!

ALI HAKIM:

No no my friend, is different.

DUNCAN:

I cannae see any difference.

9. That "whoo-whoo-whoo" sound made by movie Injuns in moments of emotional intensity.

ALI ABABWA:

Because you my friend as a member of the
dominant culture, have a totalizing and
homogenizing gaze that erases difference.

DUNCAN:

I won't have tha kind of language in my theatre!
We have a contract.

ALI ABABWA:

Yes, about the contract—

DUNCAN:

A legally binding agreement. I don't want this to
become a legal matter and I'm sure you don't
either. I prefer to speak to you as creative partners,
but I won't let you take advantage of my—of our—
broad-mindedness, our patience.

ALI HAKIM:

Please my friend, don't be angry. We'll give you
something different.

ALI ABABWA:

Mr. Manager, please, this way. Do you like
impressions?

DUNCAN:

Yes, I do.

ALI ABABWA:

Oh you're going to love this.

DUNCAN:

Is it Sean Connery?

ALI ABABWA:

Almost.

He signals the booth and leads the manager offstage.

VOICE OVER:

Ladies and gentlemen, the Secretary of Defence for the United States of America, Donald Rumsfeld.

ALI HAKIM appears in shadow on rear (tent) wall as DONALD RUMSFELD masturbating.

DONALD RUMSFELD:

Who's in power now, Hillary?!!!!!

DUNCAN:

No NO NOO!!!! Yer foul, out of bounds, disgustin'—

ALI HAKIM:

No, is beautiful. Like you and I, they are real human beings.

ALI ABABWA:

This is universal human truth.

DUNCAN:

(*to audience*) Ladies and gentlemen, please, I'm shocked, I'm shocked beyond reckoning—excuse me.

He rounds on ALI & ALI.

Look, ye, I'm trying to keep in mind that ye're a victim of the backlash but I dinnae expect to see

Donald Rumsfeld committing the sin of Onan! I've
got funders you know. They're coming to the show.
Critics. Jesus Christ—you know him?—I'm going
to get an American fatwa against me. Do you not
understand? This is not how it's done here. What
am I going to—?

ALI ABABWA:
My friend, I sense that we are having artistic
differences. Perhaps one of our embedded critics
can give you a sense of what's truly occurring.

The French Intellectual appears onscreen.

SURTITLE:
JEAN PAUL JACQUES BEAUDERRIÈREDADA
EMBEDDED CRITIC

JEAN PAUL JACQUES:
The tactic of Ali and Ali is to provoke an excess of
reality; their hypothesis is that the system itself
will commit suicide in response to multiple
deadly farts (which in the symbolic of the irreal
are pure utterances dependent on no referents).

I am French.

In this vertiginous cycle, the *jouissant* farting or
jerking off of Ali *qua* Ali provokes a critical
rupture in the discourse of power. The exchange
may be rendered thus:

PROJECTION:

$$\frac{Ali^{ali}}{Fart} \times (ticket\ price\ \partial)\ /\ authority\ index -$$
*(if/either/or + ∫audience prudishness or
confusion)*

*approx = the collapse of Western civilization
as we know it*

*Or at very least
A profound challenge to those values we hold dear*

ALI ABABWA & ALI HAKIM:
 You see?

DUNCAN:
 I'm having none a that continental codswollop.

ALI HAKIM:
 It's not codswallow. He knows. He is French.

DUNCAN:
 We're not morons. We know when we're being had,
 played around with, manipulated. I mean, if you
 were doin' a play that told us something about
 where ye came from, about your people, to
 eliminate the prejudice. But this, this fabricating
 and the pornography, it's outrageous.

 Ye've got to respect your audience. Ye understan'
 that? RESPEC'. It's part of our culture. There's
 certain things you just don't do.

ALI ABABWA:
 Oh come on, Mr. Manager, you never do this? You
 know, give quick pull in office when no one is

86

looking? (*he demonstrates*) I know I do. (*he finds a man in the audience and points him out*) I'm sure he does.

DUNCAN:

Tha's it. You people. We give ye this opportunity and ye just push our tolerance till it snaps. So, out ye get. Oot of my theatre. And you'll be hearing from my lawyer! Ladies and gentlemen, my sincerest apologies. These two will refund yer money. I'm very sorry they've wasted yer valuable time.

ALI ABABWA & ALI HAKIM:

No no no—

> *DUNCAN traps ALI HAKIM and begins to push him out of the theatre.*

ALI ABABWA:

Mr. Manager. Where are you from?

DUNCAN:

Please. The time for talk has past.

ALI ABABWA:

From Bulgaria?

DUNCAN:

(*still pushing ALI HAKIM*) Please leave.

ALI ABABWA:

From the shire.

DUNCAN:

The shire?!

ALI ABABWA:

You have hair on knuckles.

DUNCAN:

Look, ye, I'm not a bloody hobbit!

I'm a Sco'.

ALI ABABWA:

Of course ... a Sco'! Oh yes, from the fair realm of ...?

DUNCAN:

SCOTLAND, you stewpid twit!

ALI ABABWA:

Yes, Scotland. (*aside to ALI HAKIM*) I saw this movie. (*to DUNCAN*) Where the courageous and brave-hearted ...

DUNCAN:

Sco's.

ALI ABABWA:

Yes, looked death in the face against ... uh against ...

DUNCAN:

The ruthless English bastards. (*to audience*) No offence.

ALI ABABWA:
> Yes, bastards. The Sco's ... led by the brave ...
> hearted ...

DUNCAN:
> William Wallace of Elerslie!

ALI HAKIM:
> Oh, he was great hero this Walrus.

DUNCAN:
> And a true patriot. The people were with him, you
> see? And with them he resisted the cruel invader
> Edward Longshanks.

ALI ABABWA:
> Longsnacks, yes! This was the Great Battle of ...

DUNCAN:
> Falkirk!

ALI ABABWA & ALI HAKIM:
> Falkr.

ALI ABABWA:
> In the fateful year of ...

DUNCAN:
> 1298.

ALI ABABWA & ALI HAKIM:
> 1298.

> *ALI & ALI sidle back to make room for DUNCAN.*

DUNCAN:

Wallace had never before faced such an army or fought a large battle without a natural defence. He may have sensed this was the end, for he made no great exhortation, but spoke simply and bluntly to his men. "Now, I haif brocht ye to the ring—hop gif ye can!"

And at that moment the heavily mailed English cavalry fell with a tremendous shock on the charged spears of the schiltron units of the Scots.

ALI HAKIM:

Schiltron?

PHRASEOLATOR (*voice over*):

STAY AWAY FROM THE GOAT!

ALI HAKIM:

(*sotto voce*) Tim, turn that off.

ALI ABABWA:

(*to DUNCAN*) I am sorry, you were saying.

DUNCAN:

The schiltron was a fantastic device for goring and eviscerating the English dogs. No offence intended. Foot soldiers carrying 12-foot spears were arranged in tight phalanx formations. In front of these spears, great pointy stakes were hammered into the ground.

Using the schiltron, the brave-hearted Scots withstood the attack of the English dogs—no offence intended—and their Irish vassals—no offence—hammering English skulls with great battle-axes, war hammers, and the mace. Until ...

DUNCAN is momentarily overcome with emotion but then masters himself.

Red John Comyn quit the field. We were betrayed. Wallace was captured.

They dragged him around London, hanged him, then cut him down while he was still alive. Then they slit him open, pulled out his entrails and burned them before his own eyes. Then they stuck his head on a pike and placed it above London Bridge. Then they killed him. Finally, they quartered him and scattered the four pieces at Newcastle, Berwick, Aberdeen, and Perth.

DUNCAN collapses with grief, then sings.

Farewell, ye dear partners of peril! Farewell!
Though buried ye lie in one big bloody grave,
Your blood shall ennoble the place where ye fell,
And your names be enrolled with the sons of the brave![10]

DUNCAN weeps.

I cannae tell ye how that makes me feel. It's validatin' you know, to have your own people, their history, their sufferin' up here on the stage. That's what we want to see. That's why the people come. To get in touch with some basic human emotions ...

10. Adapted from a poem by Robert Tannahill (1774–1810).

ALI ABABWA:

> I know, my friend.

DUNCAN:

> This is the sort of thing that well ... you know, this
> is why we do it. *(he puts his arms around ALI & ALI)*
> I'm really proud of what we've done here. We had
> our moments, I know, our misunderstandings, but
> we persevered. We really ... I wish my mother
> could see this.

ALI HAKIM:

> You are fine actor.

DUNCAN:

> Och, it's been a long time, but yes ...

ALI ABABWA:

> Mr. Manager ...

> *DUNCAN hugs ALI ABABWA tight.*

DUNCAN:

> I love this guy.

> *Encouraged, ALI ABABWA puts his arm around the
> manager.*

ALI ABABWA:

> according to contract—

ALI HAKIM:

> Contract, right.

> *DUNCAN hugs ALI HAKIM tight.*

DUNCAN:

Love this guy too.

ALI ABABWA:

We were to have been paid, on signing, a small sum, a mere pittance really, 3 percent plus sundry minor but necessary expenses. We are in great need of this money for lodgings and food—

DUNCAN:

What are ye sayin' to me, lad? You don't think I was going to pay ye? It's different here, you know, in the West. There's nae corruption, like yer used to. Relationships here, they are built on trust. Besides, as a Sco', it hurts me, when ye imply that I'm cheap.

He leaves.

Sirens. Lights. Bells. Whistles. On-screen, MOHANDES interrupts. He is in great pain, on the verge of death.

MOHANDES:

I have been attacked. Sabotaged by terrorists ... poison on pages of *Bush at War* ... but I have located the location of the Evil aXes ...

ALI ABABWA:

Where are they Mohandes? Tell us.

MOHANDES:

At great cost-nah.

He collapses. A piece of paper falls from his hand.

ALI HAKIM:

Don't die, Mohandes.

MOHANDES gestures to the floor.

ALI ABABWA:

He's trying to tell us something.

ALI HAKIM:

They're on the floor? In the basement? Australia?

The camera zooms in on the paper. MOHANDES, making a heroic effort, turns it over. It is out of focus.

ALI ABABWA:

That paper. Perhaps is code.

ALI HAKIM:

Australia?

ALI ABABWA:

Arkansas?

ALI HAKIM:

Antigua?

ALI ABABWA:

Antilles?

ALI HAKIM:

Kuantanabongo?[11]

---

11. Agrabanian province near the Uzbeki-Lebanese border.

ALI ABABWA:
Huh?

ALI HAKIM:
Uh, Copenhagen.

We can make out the message. It reads: theatr.
ALI & ALI attempt to decipher it. They are
unsuccessful. MOHANDES rises for one last gasp.

MOHANDES:
In ... the ... audie-ence.

MOHANDES begins to die.

ALI ABABWA & ALI HAKIM:
Theatre Audience.

ALI ABABWA:
Of course.

MOHANDES continues to die.

ALI HAKIM:
Stupid us.

ALI ABABWA:
Thought you could pull one over on the blue guy.

MOHANDES is still dying.

ALI HAKIM:
I suspected it all along.

MOHANDES finally expires.

ALI ABABWA:

> TIM. Bring the jeeps.

> *TIM produces tiny white cardboard jeeps. They all suit up.*

ALI HAKIM:

> Cool helmets.

ALI ABABWA:

> Check.

ALI HAKIM:

> Ray guns.

ALI ABABWA:

> Check.

ALI HAKIM:

> Clip-on ID cards.

ALI ABABWA:

> Check.

ALI HAKIM:

> Wait, Ali Ababwa. Is this right to violate liberties of audience by entering them in this way?

ALI ABABWA:

> For sure. Ends justify means, my friend. One need only look at benefits of War on Terror for Afghanistan. 20 years ago there was dirty communist government in Kabul propped up by Soviet Union and dirty rapist heroin-smuggling warlords running the rest of the country.

ALI HAKIM:

Now there is dirty capitalist government in Kabul propped up by Americans and dirty rapist heroin-smuggling warlords still running rest of country.

ALI ABABWA:

Let us not get preoccupied with these insignificant details of the left brain.

ALI HAKIM:

You are right. TIM! This is no time for fence-sitting. Remember Mohandes.

ALL:

Huah!

They tool around in their jeeps and enter the audience.

ALI HAKIM:

Hello! We are here to investigate your Weapons of Mass Destruction, particularly the Dark aXes of el Mutah. If you do not co-operate fully, we will leave the country and you will have the shit bombed out of you. If you do co-operate fully, we will leave the country and you will have the shit bombed out of you.

ALI ABABWA:

If you actually have the aXes of Mass Destruction, however—

ALI HAKIM:

> We'll leave you alone. We represent the Coalition
> of the If You Say So. He's Mauritian. Tim's Polish.
> And I'm from Alderaan.

ALI ABABWA:

> We represent the will of a tiny percentage of the
> international community.

> *ALI HAKIM goes into the audience. Picks someone
> out. Hands him a whip.*

ALI HAKIM:

> Ah, the leader of the audience. Greetings Mr.
> President.

> *He interviews the leader.*

> Will you surrender your Weapons of Mass
> Destruction? Do you really cut off people's ears?
> Do Koreans really eat dogs? Typically cagey, their
> leader refuses to answer my probing questions.

> *Meanwhile, in another part of the audience ...*

ALI ABABWA:

> Madam, open your purse please. I am an inspector
> with the United Furniture Warehouse of Nations.
> Please, open your purse. (*to ALI HAKIM and TIM*)
> She's obfuscating.

ALI HAKIM:

> Must have something to hide. Put it in your report.

ALI ABABWA:

Semi-Colin Powell will hear about this, my dear.
You can be sure of that.

He steals the purse.

Ha! Sneaky, no? Let's see what she was hiding.

Pulls out some lipstick.

Well, it is not the aXes of Evil—but this is certainly
a weapon of mass destruction to some poor little
bunny who had it shoved up his EYEBALL!

ALI ABABWA throws the lipstick to TIM.

Tim, test the lipstick.

TIM begins to put on the lipstick.

No, no. Test the range of the lipstick.

TIM throws the lipstick.

Look—it travels further than 28 feet. That's illegal
under United Furniture Warehouse of Nations
Resolution 699, no down payment, YOU DON'T
PAY UNTIL 2010! I am confiscating this purse.

*ALI HAKIM finds a "centrifuge" next to some
innocent person.*

ALI HAKIM:

Look! A centrifuge! They mix uranium in these
things you know! How dare you! Are you not
human? Do you not think and feel the same things
we do? Tim, take this to Semi-Colin Powell. And,

fool, take my jeep and give him some water. Alert CBCNN! We will hold press conference.

Globe and Mail. No, we never said the audience *was in possession of* the Evil aXes. However, let me be perfectly clear. We believe people with white skin can govern themselves and we'll just stay here until you learn how to do so. No more questions.

A beat.

Well my friend, how 'bout now you buy me pizza? I work hard for you, yes. I drive jeeps, make joke ...?

TIM enters with a cell phone. He tries to get ALI HAKIM'S attention as ALI HAKIM attempts to get money from audience. ALI ABABWA enters from the other side and sees TIM standing there. He shoos TIM offstage.

ALI HAKIM:
I'm so hungry. You don't believe me? No? Look, my friend.

He lifts his shirt.

Listen to my stomach growl. Put your ear there.

ALI ABABWA interrupts with the cell phone.

ALI ABABWA:
Ali Hakim?

ALI HAKIM:
What? I'm busy—

ALI ABABWA:

It's Ana.

*ALI HAKIM takes the phone and speaks quietly in
Agrabanian to Ana.*

ALI ABABWA:

Ali Hakim's bride. She is phoning from detention
centre in Malta. She traded food for phone call.
They were separated in the confusion and the pig
of a smuggler took her money and instead of
taking her and her family across the mountains to
meet Ali Hakim, he drove her straight to Maltese
detention centre where she is stranded without
papers and expecting a baby in a few months. I am
to be godfather. But how will she get out? Ali
Hakim is wandering Agrabanian: stateless. He
cannot send for her. Crazy life.

ALI HAKIM:

Ali Ababwa. The baby is kicking.

ALI ABABWA:

Tell Ana to take care of herself. She must eat for
two. Not waste food on phone calls.

He turns back to audience.

Look at Ali Hakim, he is smiling. Oh my friend is
a lucky man.

*ALI HAKIM goes offstage to continue his call in
private. ALI ABABWA tiptoes to centre stage.*

So. I'm single, pretty smart, sometimes amusing
and somewhat exotic. I like long walks, dancing a

bit strangely, and going to the theatre if I can leave at intermission. When they have an intermission.

On the liability side, my bum is more or less constantly sore and though I have no children of my own (*sighs*), I do have dependents, many dependents, all of whom depend on me to send money home to buy food, water, and medicine.

He sings an excerpt from "I Want to Be Loved by You."

So—any takers? Ian, what do you say? Is OK, I am very open-minded. No, you are right. Two famous handsome brown men in one household—it would be all ego.

He picks a woman from the audience and approaches her.

How about you, madam? What do you say? Is easy, if immigration interrogates you, all you have to do is convince them of our intimacy. And believe me, once you've had Agrabanian you never go back. Please. I don't want to go back.

He retreats.

Oh, sure. Typical. You Canadians. You're so nice and liberal and I support same-sex marriages and when you walk down the street and see a woman with a dot on her forehead, you think that's pretty cool and maybe you even have dot envy. But when it comes to blue Agrabanians, well that's a whole different story now, isn't it? Oh, yes you believe blue Agrabanians should share the same rights and privileges as you and no you would never discriminate against blue Agrabanians and yes you think hate-crimes legislation should be rewritten to include blue Agrabanians but do you think blue is sexxxxxyyyy?

He returns to the woman.

Kiss me and I'll shut up. Is true. Just one. On the cheek. Blue is permanent—won't come off on lips, I promise.

Ad-libbing as necessary until she—or he—does.

(*after kiss*) Be still my beating heart.

VOICE OVER:
According to Agrabanian Traditional Law, if a woman kisses a man they are deemed to have been married since they were 13—and all property reverts to the male.

ALI ABABWA:
May I have keys to late model luxury sedan? Credit card? You will find that I can adapt quickly to your carefree lifestyle. Please, I beg you, take me with you.

Enter ALI HAKIM.

ALI HAKIM:
What are you doing? Madam, people, please, there is no such thing as traditional law in Agraba.

ALI ABABWA:
Ha! Just a joke.

ALI HAKIM:

You have no shame, no respect.

ALI ABABWA:

What? Is part of show.

ALI HAKIM:

You think I can't hear you from back there? You want to stay here then. For real.

ALI ABABWA:

Ali Hakim.

ALI HAKIM:

You will just forget us? Forget Ana, forget Souad? Me?

Silence.

You forget who you are.

ALI ABABWA turns away angrily from ALI HAKIM.

Roll video please.

PROJECTION:
A map of Agraba.

PROJECTION:
Agraba: A People's History.

ALI HAKIM:

Ladies and gentlemen: Agraba has a long and complicated and beautiful history but I will only tell you of the Agraba we grew up in. Agraba was a country of few haves and many have-nots. The "government" was a corrupt oligarchy supported by imperial powers who controlled Agraba's agronium mines.

1968. In comes Agraba's great reformer: Jafar Ali Salim, head of the Agronium Miner's Union, who calls for a nationwide general strike.

PROJECTION:
The Agrabanian Flag.

I remember getting up in the morning to find my father still at home and I said to him, "Poopa, what is wrong? Why are you at home?" And he explained to me that he was not going to work, he was on strike. For as long as I could remember my mother and father were always worrying about money and whether my father's job would last and there they were jeopardizing everything.

The strike went on for months. Everybody went out in the end. Almost everybody. The general strike was the watershed. The oligarchy—

ALI ABABWA:

(*sotto voce*) donkey shitters—

ALI HAKIM:

collapsed. And Jafar Ali Salim became Agraba's first democratically elected leader. What days those were. The conversations. The poetry. The music. The street corner debates. The promise.

For first time ever, agronium profits stay in country. Healthcare is free. Education is free. University. This is where I meet Ali Ababwa. He is leader of student union. We are in charge of our country, our lives, he says in big speech. We must work to make our future happen. Everyone claps, cheers.

ALI ABABWA:
This was long time ago, Ali Hakim.

ALI HAKIM:
He had hippy clothes. Big hair. (*beat*) That's when you met Souad. Remember?

ALI ABABWA:
I remember.

A moment of silence.

ALI HAKIM:
Of course it couldn't last.

ALI ABABWA:
The Sammites

ALI HAKIM:
backed by the CIA

ALI ABABWA:
started to make trouble.

ALI HAKIM:
Then the coup d'état.

ALI ABABWA:
Jafar Ali Salim died defending our revolution.

ALI HAKIM:

> His soul ascended to the golden shores of Piña Majorca.

ALI ABABWA:

> You can be sure.

ALI ABABWA & ALI HAKIM:

> May we all find ourselves in Piña.

> *They make the Piña Majorca gesture.*

ALI HAKIM:

> With Jafar. And Souad.

> *ALI ABABWA nods in acknowledgement.*

ALI ABABWA:

> The Sammite extremists established the Theocratic State of Agraba.

ALI HAKIM:

> These clerics who had renounced the material world were now driven around in the latest model Mercedes, and lived in palatial homes waited on hand and foot.

ALI ABABWA:

> People got together and tried to resist this new alliance between the clerics and the oligarchy. Who knows how things might have worked out?

ALI HAKIM:

> But then came the business with the flight schools and the Thin Towers and the need to vaporize

every tent in Afghanistan. And while you were all watching Gulf War 2: The Sequel on CBCNN, the U.S.A. launched top-secret mission Operation Agrabust. Under U.S. command, coalition troops from Mauritius and the Solomon Islands invaded Agraba and seized control one more time.

ALI ABABWA:
Of the agronium mines and the water.

ALI HAKIM:
Of the palaces and remnants of the CIA-trained secret police.

ALI ABABWA:
Of the decayed power plants and children begging in the streets.

ALI HAKIM:
Opening up an exciting emerging market. Today in Agraba City is two-mile line-up for gasoline. They say is liberation and they close newspapers and blow up hospitals, sell off national industries. Call it reconstruction. Put up shiny new fence of barbed wire around my sister's village. No one is allowed to come or go without permission of provisional authority. When my sister complain, they bulldoze her house. I haven't heard from her since.

Today in Agraba City, the same religious police who murdered Ali Ababwa's Souad now make successful applications to Provisional Authority for lots of new guns.

ALI ABABWA:

Is a very big mess, my friends.

ALI HAKIM:

Very big.

A moment of quiet then music sneaks in. They sing the national anthem of Agraba.

ALI ABABWA & ALI HAKIM:

Oh I'm proud to be Agrabanian
There's no food but there's lots of tea
And I won't forget all the men
From whom I bummed smokes for free

My country's two kilometres
From sea to oily sea
Thank God for our Agraba
And my sister's black-and-white TV

Please join us ...

On-screen, a karaoke version begins.

I'm proud to be Agrabanian
Not a stinking Turkish dog
I love to eat the chickpea
And have forsworn the hog

Oh Agraba, oh Agraba
Long live the green and chrome
'Til we get to Piña Majorca
Our one and only home

ALI ABABWA & ALI HAKIM:

May we all find ourselves in Piña.

They do the Piña Majorca gesture.

ALI ABABWA:
I need a break.

ALI ABABWA leaves.

ALI HAKIM:
So do I. TIM!

TIM enters.

(*glaring at audience*) Keep an eye on them. Make sure they don't try to steal anything. If they do, it comes out of your pay, Tim.

ALI HAKIM leaves. A long pause.

TIM:
It's *Tom*. My *name* is Tom.

He turns to audience.

I'm sorry about this. I'm not responsible—these guys they, well you've seen how they treat me. I'm a professional actor. I did the *X-Files*. Two episodes.

PROJECTION:
A scene from X-Files *with Tom Butler in it.*[12]

I worked with Meryl Streep.

PROJECTION:
A scene from Meryl Streep movie with Tom Butler in it.

---

12. If an actor playing Tim has suitable film, TV, or video credits, they can be substituted. If not, some other device might be called for.

I did two feature films in China.

PROJECTION:
A scene from Chinese movie with Tom Butler.

Freddy vs. Jason.

PROJECTION:
A scene from Freddy vs. Jason *with Tom Butler in it.*

I was in *Josie and the Pussy Cats.*

PROJECTION:
A scene from Josie and the Pussy Cats *with Tom Butler in it.*

Did you see that? Maybe your kids saw it? I love kids. Making them laugh.

He pulls out the Ali and Ali promotional postcard.

But you know, there's no work. The Keep It in America campaign is just killing us up here and stupid us for never developing our own industry and always relying on the Americans. Like we thought they wouldn't abandon us when things got tough or the dollar went too high? And now the Terminator is governor.

So, I'm reduced to this. Working for these two ... just to put food in my daughter's horse's stable.

PROJECTION:
TIM'S daughter's horse.

I love the theatre. I studied at the National Theatre School. You know I was around in the original TWP days. Been doing this a while. But these two they're ... I don't know what kind of Muslims they're supposed to be; they're always trying to get me to buy them martinis. And that Blue One, I don't know, I don't think it's real, the blue. And the play ... There's so much they could be doing with this material: I mean really showing the suffering and exposing the connections of the American elite, you know George W. and Arbusto Energy; Dick Cheney and Haliburton Oil; Condoleezza Rice and Chevron; she even has an oil tanker named after her. And Poindexter and Abrams getting a pardon for Iran-Contra. And did you hear about the Bush administration insuring American corporations in Iraq with taxpayers' money, because the private companies are too smart to take the risk? That's how we would have done it at TWP—

ALI & ALI return.

ALI ABABWA:

What are you doing, fool? Shut up. Is the name of this show, *Tim and Tim and the aXes of Evil*? No. It's *Ali and Ali and the aXes of Evil*. Shut up. Off.

TIM protests. ALI HAKIM produces a black hood, such as was used by U.S. soldiers on inmates at Abu Ghraib prison (and probably elsewhere).

TIM:

No, please, not the hood. I'm not gonna wear that again.

ALI HAKIM escorts TIM off.

ALI ABABWA:

Don't mind him, he's from Ottawa. Now, ladies and gentlemen, as we approach the end of our show we are very pleased to welcome onto the stage our newest, no, our very first corporate sponsor. You know we asked a lot of people for support and, surprisingly, not many were interested. We asked, for example, CAE, big Canadian weapons manufacturer. We thought it was a good fit. They make all those weapons being used where we come from and the show is all about that but they weren't interested. Not even a postcard.[13]

ALI HAKIM runs on excitedly.

ALI HAKIM:

He's here! I brought him out of the taxi myself.

ALI ABABWA:

Ladies and gentlemen, please join us in extending a warm clash of civilizations welcome to the president of Al Qaeda, Mr. Osama bin Laden.

OSAMA enters. He is carrying an AK-47 and a suitcase.

OSAMA:

Thank you very much. Begging your indulgence, I am Osama bin Laden and I am the leader of Al Qaeda.

---

13. They also asked Saddam Hussein, who *was* interested, but unfortunately he'd had a bad year and felt this wasn't the right time for him to give.

From the beginning, art has been a part of all our lives. Or so I am told. As a Wahabbi, I take a dim view of art, among other things. But, hey, I am willing to try something new. As Omar the Mullah likes to say, "You take what you can get before you get to the virgins."

It is not enough to blow up big buildings once every ten years. We must win the hearts and minds of the infidel. It is for this reason that we have begun our first strategic partnership with the poor and downtrodden members of Canada's artistic community.

And so, Dan, on behalf of Al Qaeda, I'm very pleased to present Ali and Ali with this gift to support your production *The Adventures of Ali and Ali and the Taxis of Evil.*

He hands over the suitcase.

ALI ABABWA:
Actually, it's the aXes of Evil.

OSAMA:
Yes. Congratulations.

ALI & ALI look at the audience.

ALI ABABWA:
What? You don't like our sponsor?

ALI HAKIM:
Mr. ...

OSAMA:
Call me Osama.

ALI HAKIM:
Please, small moment.

OSAMA checks his watch then sits. They all sit on rug together.

Though it may come as a surprise to you, most people in these parts perceive Al Qaeda as a loose band of unwashed murderous terrorists who also like to oppress women.

OSAMA rants in fundamentalist gibberish.

ALI ABABWA:
No no no. That stuff has got to stop.

OSAMA:
Stop jihad?

ALI ABABWA:
Great.

ALI HAKIM:
Sure.

OSAMA:
Never! (*more fundamentalist gibberish*)

ALI ABABWA:
OK, it's OK if you don't want to stop jihad because, from what we can tell, here in the postmodern,

post-industrial West, it is not your actions that count so much as your image.

ALI HAKIM:

Perhaps what you are facing is image problem.

ALI ABABWA:

No no, perceptual challenge.

ALI HAKIM:

Many groups have them.

ALI ABABWA:

Monsanto, for example.

ALI HAKIM:

Pfizer.

ALI ABABWA:

Shell.

ALI HAKIM:

Dow Chemical.

ALI ABABWA:

Or GE. Making and selling all those weapons to Israel, Kuwait, and Egypt. How many people do they kill?

ALI HAKIM:

Or Lockheed Martin, maker of F-16. How many people do they kill?

ALI ABABWA:

Or Raytheon. Maker of wide variety of missile. How many people do they kill?

ALI HAKIM:

Or Ronald Reagan. Or Madeleine Albright and Bill Clinton. How many people did they kill? Or Henry Kissinger.[14]

ALI ABABWA:

How many people did he kill?

ALI HAKIM:

Like you, a very rich man and also wanted in several countries.

ALI ABABWA:

Just as these shady individuals and organizations utilize the tools of public relations to minimize the consequences of their crimes so too can you and your organization, Mr. Osama.

ALI HAKIM:

Perhaps they need a new name.

14. The revision of history was in full swing when we performed in Edmonton (June 2004) and so we added some names to respond to events. Ronald Reagan had finally died and was (virtually) everywhere being hailed as a great man who had brought peace and stability to the globe. His responsibility for the U.S.-sponsored terrorist war on Nicaragua in the 1980s (along with his war on the poor) was conveniently dumped in the Memory Hole.

Madeleine Albright, you may recall, was Clinton's Secretary of State who, when asked how she felt about the half a million Iraqi children dying as a result of U.S.-imposed sanctions (after the First War on Iraq), answered, "It's a tough choice but we think it's worth it."

ALI ABABWA:

Al Qaeda has a lot of negative connotations.

ALI HAKIM:

But I don't think he wants to give up Al Qaeda altogether.

ALI ABABWA:

Top marks for visibility.

ALI HAKIM:

You can't buy that kind of recognition.

ALI ABABWA:

But you could, you know—change it.

ALI HAKIM:

Make it fresh.

ALI ABABWA:

Different.

ALI HAKIM:

New.

ALI ABABWA:

New Al Qaeda!

ALI HAKIM:

New is good. But also kind of old. How about Al Qaeda 2.0.? Or AQ2.

ALI ABABWA:

Yes! You know it's Al Qaeda but you don't.

ALI HAKIM:

And easier to spell.

ALI ABABWA:

Besides you're already doing lots of things right.

> *PROJECTION:*
> *A flow chart that lays out the bin Ladens' numerous*
> *connections to American politicians and Industrialists*
> *(and Celine Dion). Not to mention the role the*
> *Illuminati play at Six Flags Amusement Park as*
> *well as the attendance of Henry Kissinger at Lord*
> *and Lady Black's Christmas party.*

ALI ABABWA:

Come on out of the cave! Make a virtue out of your connections. You know—how your family does business with the Bushes, how your family invests in Bechtel, which is making pretty good coin on Iraqi reconstruction.

Sure, my client drove some big planes into some tall buildings but who here hasn't made mistakes.

ALI HAKIM:

Like U.S.A.—getting into bed with Shah of Iran, with Saddam Hussein, with Taliban. These are mistakes anyone can make.

ALI ABABWA:

You say—whoops—is all different now.

ALI HAKIM:

You could still win the Nobel Peace Prize.

ALI ABABWA:

Like Henry Kissinger.

ALI HAKIM:

Or Peres, Rabin, and Arafat.

ALI ABABWA:

But to get to this level I think you also need to re-brand *yourself.*

ALI HAKIM:

Osama bin Laden?

ALI ABABWA:

Unh nuh nuh.

ALI HAKIM:

How about ... Osama bin ... Oprah.

ALI ABABWA:

Ahhhh! Yin and yang.

ALI HAKIM:

New and old.

ALI ABABWA:

Black and kind of yellow. It appeals to a broad spectrum. Good, no?

OSAMA:

No.

ALI HAKIM:

OK. You're right. Goodbye—thanks for the briefcase. Can we apply two years in a row?

OSAMA:

(*off*) Omar, quick, bring the taxi.

ALI HAKIM:

Let's see how much Osama left us, shall we?

They pick up the briefcase. It's heavy. Ticking is heard. ALI & ALI turn to the audience, questioning. They turn to each other.

There is a lengthy, deafening, and terrifying explosion. Lights blind the audience.

VOICE OVER:

Ladies and gentlemen, please remain seated. This is not a real explosion; it is only theatre, an illusion. There is no immediate danger to you. Please stick around and buy a commemorative programme, have a drink in the upstairs bar. We repeat: this is not a real explosion.

The actor who plays TIM/OSAMA appears in a pool of light, peeling off his Osama beard and moustache.

TIM:

(*overlapping*) We repeat: this is not a real explosion. Had this been a real explosion from, say, a 5,000-pound Laser Guided Penetrator Smart Bomb or a 22-year-old Chechen widow with 6 kilograms of explosives strapped to her body, you would not be hearing this announcement. Your children would have been left father- or motherless, any friends living in the immediate vicinity would have been wiped out. We repeat: this is not real. Look, there you are. There's your hand, still good for taking your daughter's hand, writing a poem, scratching your bum. There's your lover, your friend, your dad, a stranger beside you. You see. It's only an illusion.

The lights shift to reveal ALI HAKIM smoking a hookah while ALI ABABWA prepares for bed.

ALI HAKIM:
(*singing to himself*)
This is the end
My Semitic Friend, the end
Of our elaborate plans, the end

He turns to the audience.

It really is. The end. Thank you for coming.

He sings again.

I'll never look into her eyes again.

ALI ABABWA:
Don't be so pessimistic.

He removes his "show" shirt and puts on a t-shirt.

ALI HAKIM:
I'm hungry.

ALI ABABWA:
Have a smoke, it dulls the hunger.

To audience.

Ah, good night. We're going to ... Ali Hakim, they're just sitting there.

ALI HAKIM shrugs.

ALI ABABWA:
My bum hurts.

ALI HAKIM:
Have a smoke. It dulls the pain.

ALI ABABWA:
Really, this is the only thing, just to sit quietly, like this.

ALI HAKIM:
Ali Ababwa ... you are really wishing to stay here with them?

ALI ABABWA:
I don't know, Ali Hakim. (*a pause*) I don't know—

He notices ALI HAKIM has fallen asleep. He turns to the audience.

When you decide to go, please leave quietly as Ali Hakim is sleeping. Good night.

He draws on the narguilah. His eyes close. The light dims. Music (Souad Massi) plays. They wake.

ALI HAKIM:
Ali Ababwa.

ALI ABABWA:
Ali Hakim.

They see the audience and realize they were dreaming.

ALI HAKIM:
I had the most

ALI ABABWA:
beautiful dream.

ALI HAKIM:
I was at my sister's house

ALI ABABWA:
back in Agraba.

ALI HAKIM:
Only the whole world was Agraba.

ALI ABABWA:
And everyone was there. You

They "see" these people in the audience; they tell their dream to the house.

ALI HAKIM:
Ana

ALI ABABWA:
Souad was alive.

ALI HAKIM:
Spring had come.

ALI ABABWA:
The snow melted

ALI HAKIM:
and the village overflowed

ALI ABABWA:
with children.

ALI HAKIM:
Our words had grown taller than our swords.

ALI ABABWA:
The battlefields were green with grass.

ALI HAKIM:
And everyone had meaningful work.

ALI ABABWA:
And food enough.

ALI HAKIM:
And clean water.

ALI ABABWA:
And it was all

ALI HAKIM:
so easy

ALI ABABWA:
so simple.

A beat.

ALI ABABWA:
This must have been Piña Majorca.

ALI HAKIM:

No, Ali, I think perhaps it was the future.

ALI ABABWA looks to ALI HAKIM as the lights fade to black.

The End.